Contents

Richmond

A Practical Guide
for Visitors

Compiled by Malcolm Boyes

Illustrated by J. J. Thomlinson

DALESMAN BOOKS
1982

The Dalesman Publishing Company Ltd.,
Clapham, via Lancaster, LA2 8EB.

First published 1978

Second edition 1982

ISBN: 0 85206 680 5

Printed in Great Britain by
George Todd & Son, Marlborough Street, Whitehaven

Introduction

RICHMOND has many of the features and customs people expect of a market town, and few can equal. The castle keep overshadows the cobbled Market Square. In the same way as Knaresborough castle stands on a crag above the river Nidd, Richmond castle overlooks the river Swale. Ripon and York both have their distinctive customs and so has Richmond. The curfew bell is still rung from Holy Trinity church, and the passing bell mourns the dead of the town. The town clerk has to be approved by the Queen; the mayor has a special box in the unique Georgian Theatre; and every seven years the boundaries of Richmond are ridden.

The town has given its name to many other Richmonds all over the world. There were over 50 at the last count. There are Richmonds in Africa, Australia and over 30 on the American continent, and nearer home, in Ireland, Scotland and Surrey. About half these towns submitted pictures of themselves for an exhibition in 1971 celebrating 900 years since the founding of Richmond castle.

Richmond has for many years been a garrison town. It is a fitting tribute that the Green Howards Museum is now established in the old Holy Trinity church. The parish church also has a chapel to the Green Howards and two Books of Remembrance. The main road south to the A1 passes through Catterick Camp, the modern military garrison. The town makes a fine touring base, situated at the foot of Swaledale with Wensleydale and Teesdale within easy reach.

General Information

Richmond is in North Yorkshire, formerly the North Riding of Yorkshire. It is situated on the river Swale at the foot of Swaledale. The town is 4 miles from the A1 at Scotch Corner, 12 miles from Darlington, 27 miles from Teesside, 49 miles from Leeds, 45 miles from Newcastle and 234 miles from London.

Population: 7,500 approx.

Bus services: United Bus Company operates services to Leyburn - Aysgarth - Hawes, Reeth - Keld, Scorton - Darlington, Bedale, Northallerton, Catterick Camp and local services.

Car parks: Hurgill Road, Riverside Road, Nuns Close car park and Newbiggen.

Coach park: Near The Green.

Toilets: Banks Yard, off the Market Place; Victoria Street, near Friary Gardens; The Green; Riverside Walk and Nuns Close car park.

Street plan: Market Place, near Trinity church; and Friary Gardens.

Map: 1 inch to the mile map on Trinity church (Green Howards Museum).

Police station: I'Anson Road. Phone 2245 or 3055.

Post office: Queens Road, opposite Friary Gardens. Sub post offices at Westfields, Gilling Road and Cutpurse.

Banks: National Westminster, Barclays, Midland, Yorkshire and York County Savings.

Churches:
Church of England—St. Mary's Parish Church, Station Road; St. Agatha's Church, Easby.
Methodist—Queens Road.
Roman Catholic—SS Joseph Francis Xavier, Newbiggen.
United Reform—Dundas Street.
Pentecostal Church—Castle Hill.

Information Bureau: Friary Gardens.

Early Closing Day: Wednesday.

Market Day: Saturday.

Library: Dundas Street.

Swimming Pool: Recreation Centre, off Station Road.

Cinema: Zetland, Victoria Road.

Golf: 18 hole course open to the public daily, Gallowgate, Richmond.

Angling: Fishing permits from Metcalfe's Sports Shop, Market Place; The Bungalow, Easby Abbey; Mr. Carter, Swale View Caravan Site, Reeth Road, Richmond.

Bowls: Ronaldshay Park, Quaker Lane, open daily 11 a.m. till dusk.

Horse racing: Catterick (3 miles), Flat and National Hunt.

Caravan sites: Swale View Caravan Park, Reeth Road; Hargill House, Gilling West.

Picnic site: Round Howe, Reeth Road (National Trust).

Children's playing field: Quaker Lane.

Newspaper: *Darlington and Stockton Times, Richmond and Catterick Advertiser*, issued free, fortnightly.

The market cross

THE MARKET PLACE

THIS is the centre of Richmond, all the roads radiating out from the square, although the main road is diverted away. The square is dominated by Holy Trinity church and the obelisk which replaced the market cross. The original market cross was a handsome structure with a square platform set at the top of a flight of steps, above which was an ornamental cross surrounded by a six feet high wall. The four buttresses each carried a carved stone dog. Criminals were flogged after being fastened to two rings set in the north-east pillar. On one occasion, when an Irishman and a Scotsman were sentenced to be flogged, the Scotsman begged as a favour to have a piece of canvas on his back. The magistrate granted the request and asked the Irishman if he would like a favour. In a broad Irish accent he replied: 'If it pleases your honour, I'd like the Scotsman on my back while I'm being flogged!' This favour wasn't granted. Nearby stood the pillory and three crosses where wheat, barley and oats were sold.

Holy Trinity church, which now houses the Green Howards Museum, is unique in once having had shops in the north aisle. It has had a chequered history since it was built about 1150. After a while it became too small and the present parish church was erected outside the town walls. The church fell into ruins and was rebuilt in 1360, but was again in ruins by 1439. When the plague visited Richmond in 1597 and 1598 it was used as a refuge. It has also been used as a warehouse for storing beer and other goods, as a school, a town hall and an assize court. In the 1890s there was a dwelling house and a tobacconist's shop between the steeple and the nave!

The curfew bell is still rung from the tower, the tradition possibly dating back to William I. It was originally rung at 8 o'clock at night, so that the inhabitants could put out their fires, bolt their doors, and retire in order to be up at six when the bell was sounded again. In recent years the rising bell has been rung at 8 o'clock, a concession to more civilised times. Other traditional ringings included the pancake bell, which can still be heard at 11 o'clock on Shrove Tuesday. Two other peals could be requested by Richmond folk; the passing bell signalled a death—nine bells for a man, six for a woman and three for a child—and the gathering peal summoned mourners to the funeral.

Surrounding the cobbled Market Place is a wide variety of shops and hotels. The Kings Head has a fine sign showing King Charles II. At the other side of the square is the Bishop Blaize Hotel, propably Richmond's oldest surviving inn. The sign above the door shows Bishop Blaize with a crozier in one hand and a woolcomb in the other. The patron saint of woolcombers, he was an Armenian bishop who was martyred in 316 A.D. The inn was the centre of the knitting and making-up industry, the first pair of stockings made here reputedly being given to Queen Elizabeth I in 1560. At the top of the Market Place is T. Haywood & Sons, boot-makers and footwear specialists. There is often an interesting display of old photographs and other items about the town tastefully arranged around the boots and shoes in the win-dow.

THE GREEN HOWARDS MUSEUM

THE museum was opened on July 25th, 1973, by King Olav V of Norway, the Colonel-in-Chief of the regiment. In the foyer can be seen two 6-pounder field guns of 1795, which were privately made and used by the Loyal Dales Volunteers. The ground floor is devoted to uniforms and other items connected with the North Riding Volunteers from 1795 to 1907. On the upper ground floor are more uniforms of the Green Howards and North Riding Militia. On the first floor is the regimental plate and the collection of plate belonging to the Borough of Richmond, as well as the medal room containing many of the campaign and gallantry medals awarded to the Green Howards. The museum has three George Crosses and nine of the eighteen V.C.s awarded to the regiment's officers and men. There are over 2,000 medals on display from every campaign and war that the Green Howards has been in since the Crimean War.

On the second floor is the story of the regiment from its founding in 1688 to the present day. There are exhibits from the many small campaigns, from the War of Austrian Succession in 1745 to Malaya in 1952, and also from the Crimean War, the Boer War and the two World Wars. To convert the church into this fine museum cost £90,000, most of the money being raised within the regiment. The work involved was recognised when it was awarded the runner's-up prize in the 1975 National Heritage Museum of the Year competition.

RICHMOND CASTLE

THERE is a fine view down to the river Swale from the castle, which is thought to have been built in 1071 by Alan the Red. It was never besieged but may, as with many Yorkshire towns, have been attacked by Scottish raiding parties. Two Scottish kings have been imprisoned within the castle; William the Lion was kept here until a ransom of £100,000 was paid, and David II was held in 1346 after being captured at the Battle of Neville's Cross. He was later taken to Odiham Castle in Hampshire while the ransom was being raised. Charles I was brought here in 1646, a prisoner on his way to Holmby House.

The entrance to the castle is through a gateway at the side of the barbican, which once had a portcullis. After paying a small charge you enter the Great Court, an area of neatly trimmed grass. If you look back at the gatehouse you can see the military prison which is no longer in use. Turn right and visit the base of the keep; it rises to a height of 100 feet and in the central pillar is a well. A spiral staircase in one corner winds up to the floor above, but this may become congested and an easier way is to turn left out of the keep and climb the stairway twenty yards in front of you. A straight stairway then leads to a hall, from where more steps go to the top of the keep. There is a fine view down into the Market Place below and across the rooftops of Richmond to the surrounding countryside. On the way up the stairways there are interesting glimpses of the town through the slit windows.

When you return to the Great Court turn left. Following the wall you pass Robin Hood's Tower, where it is thought

William the Lion was imprisoned. In the corner of the Great
Court, which forms a huge triangle, is Gold Hole Tower,
connected with a tradition concerning buried treasure. In
this corner were the main domestic buildings—the kitchen,
chapel and Scoland's Hall on the upper floor, the room
below probably being a store. Turning right along the edge
of the Great Court, you get an extremely fine view of the
river Swale and Richmond Bridge. On the western wall, as
you return to the gatehouse, is a plaque: 'Robert Baden
Powell, Founder of the Scout and Guide Movement, lived
here from 1908–1910 in the barracks which formerly stood
on this site.'

KING ARTHUR AND POTTER THOMPSON

THERE is a tradition that King Arthur and his knights of
the Round Table are sleeping under Richmond Castle,
waiting to be called when England needs them. Many years
ago a local man called Potter Thompson was walking alongside the river Swale, beneath the castle, when his discovered
an underground cave. He ventured down the passage and
eventually came into a vast hall. All around the room were
large men, clad in armour, with their swords and shields
nearby—all were breathing but asleep. On a stone table was
a sword in a jewelled scabbard and a gold and ivory horn.
Looking around the room he recognised King Arthur by his
crown. He now wanted proof of his visit so he picked up
the sword and the sleeping knights began to stir. He replaced
the sword and picked up the horn but again the knights
stirred. This was too much; he took to his heels down the
passage, and as he ran a voice sang out:

> *Potter, Potter Thompson,*
> *If thou hadst either drawn*
> *The sword or blown the horn,*
> *Thou'd been the luckiest man*
> *That ever yet was born!*

When he returned later to find the underground passage it
had disappeared.

CASTLE WALK

THE Castle Walk is a fine footpath which runs at the base of the castle walls. Leave the Market Place by the road beside the Talbot Hotel. Don't descend the hill but bear left along cobbled Castle Hill. On the right, across the valley, is Culloden Tower. The broad footpath skirts the outside of the castle with a steep drop down to the river Swale. Beneath the crags and masonry which defend this side of the castle are a number of seats where you can sit and admire the fine view. As you leave Castle Walk you can see the keep in front of you. Return back to the Market Place by carrying straight on along Millgate.

RICHMONDSHIRE MUSEUM

TUCKED away in Ryders Wynd, to the north of the Market Place, is the new Richmondshire Museum. It is easily reached by turning left along Frenchgate at the bottom of the Market Place and taking the first turn left — the museum is set back on the right. Housed in a two-storey building is a growing collection of ephemera and postcards relating to Richmond. There are numerous photographs, including some of the time when the town was a popular cyclists' rendezvous, models, outdated tools and equipment, old maps and many other items offering visitors a fascinating glimpse at the Richmond of yesteryear.

FRIARS WYND AND GREYFRIARS PRIORY

FRIARS WYND is a passage which leaves the Market Place alongside the shop of C. Hodgson & Sons. Half-way down is an archway, originally a postern gate allowing easy access between the Market Place and the church of Greyfriars. Beside it you can still see a portion of the town wall, which was also pierced by three bars at Frenchgate, Finkle Street and Bargate. Continuing through the archway you can see the tower of Greyfriars church straight in front of you. The

tower is all that was completed of a new church before the
Dissolution of the Monasteries. In the grounds of the Franciscan monastery was the only well, apart from the two in
the castle, so there would be a regular traffic of people coming
through Friars Wynd for water. There are some beautiful
gardens beneath the tower and a number of seats on which
to rest. The Tourist Information Bureau is also situated in
the gardens.

THE GEORGIAN THEATRE

OPPOSITE the Priory Gardens is the unpretentious building
which houses the unique Richmond Theatre. To be taken
on a tour of it is like stepping back two centuries. In 1787
an actor manager, Samuel Butler, suggested to Richmond
Corporation that it should erect a proper theatre. Butler
created a northern touring circuit linking theatres in Ripon,
Harrogate, Northallerton, Beverley and Kendal, and moved
props and scenery by cart between the theatres!

The prices charged seem dear for the late 18th century.
The boxes were three shillings, the pit two shillings and the
gallery one shilling. When a star actor appeared the prices
went up to four shillings for the boxes and best rows in the
pit and three shillings for the rest of the pit. In 1808 a
young boy called Carey joined Samuel Butler's touring company. He later moved on to London and became the famous
actor Edmund Kean, who performed again at Richmond
—the playbill on September 6th, 1819 can still be seen inside
the theatre. There are many more interesting playbills and
photographs decorating the walls, as well as the autographs
of distinguished visitors including the Queen Mother, the
Duke and Duchess of Kent, Dame Edith Evans and Dame
Sybil Thorndyke.

When you step into the pit the first impression is of the
small size of the theatre, although the seating capacity is
somehow 237 people. The boxes around the pit carry the
names of famous playwrights such as Shakespeare and
Dryden, and on the pillars are the two bracket candleholders which illuminate the place. The mayor's box, on
the right, bears the town's coat of arms. There are peep

holes in the doors to enable the manager to keep an eye on his audience!

To look at the fine theatre now you wouldn't think that 40 years ago it was a salvage depot. In the 1820s and '30s the audiences declined, and in 1848 the theatre became an auction room. Sometime after this the two levels were sealed off, leaving two separate places. For a hundred years the building was used for an assortment of jobs—the cellars for storing wine and the upper floor as a corn chandler's store and a furniture repository. In 1960 an appeal was launched by the Georgian Theatre (Richmond) Trust Ltd., and two years later the theatre was opened to the public. It is very much a live theatre with a series of performances each year. At other times it is open daily to visitors. What was once a warehouse and wine cellar is now the finest Georgian theatre in Europe.

Richmond Bridge from Castle Walk

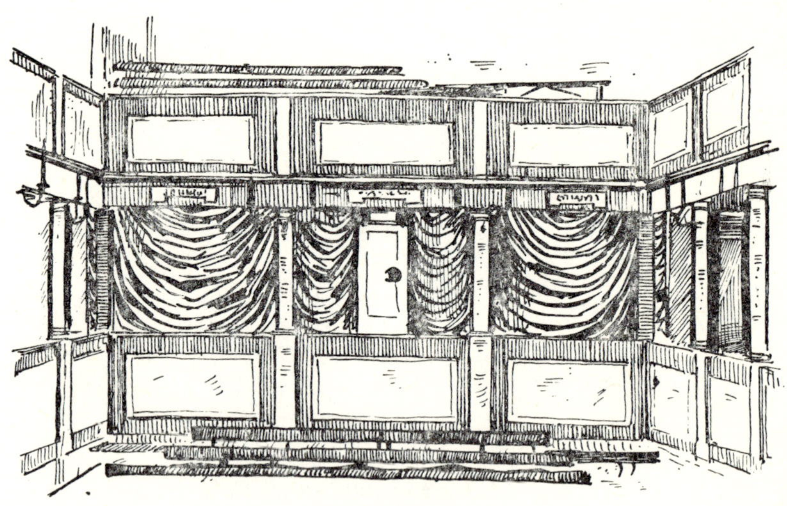

Exterior and interior views of the
Gorgian Theatre

16

STATION ROAD, ST. MARY'S CHURCH AND FRENCHGATE

FROM the bottom end of the Market Place turn left along Frenchgate and then down Station Road, the first turn on the right. On your right, opposite the entrance to the church, is Richmond Grammar School, now comprehensive. There was a grammar school in Richmond in 1392, which was reorganised and endowed by the corporation in the reign of Queen Elizabeth I, and was situated in the parish churchyard. The present school you see was built in 1850 as a memorial to Canon Tate, a great educationalist and the headmaster from 1796 to 1833. One of the most famous pupils was Charles Lutwidge Dodgson who became an Oxford Don and is better known as Lewis Caroll, author of *Alice in Wonderland.*

Station Road continues down to Station Bridge, renamed Mercury Bridge in 1975 to commemorate the 50th anniversary of the Royal Corps of Signals being stationed in Catterick. There is a plaque at the far end. On the left, at the other side of the bridge, is the old railway station, now a garden and farming centre. Close by is the new heated indoor swimming pool, opened in 1976.

Opposite the grammar school is St. Mary's parish church, restored in 1858. The tower and north porch are 15th century, but a few parts date back to the 12th century. Inside there is an interesting old alms box, and on the capital of the first pillar, on the right, is a carving of a sheep. In the chancel are the finely carved stalls from Easby Abbey which were placed here after the Dissolution of the Monasteries. Underneath the third seat on the right is a misericord depicting a pig playing the bagpipes while two other pigs dance. There are a number of plaques and brasses to soldiers in the church. On the right of the chancel is the Regimental Chapel of the Green Howards, in which all the woodwork is carved by Robert Thompson of Kilburn—try finding the mouse which is his trademark. The carved wooden altar piece shows soldiers in action. On either side of the altar is a Book of Remembrance recording the men of the Green Howards who gave their lives in two World Wars. A page of each book is turned every week. There are also 23 regimental colours dating from 1801 laid up in the chapel.

The churchyard has a number of interesting gravestones. As you approach it from Church Wynd you see between the paths a stone to Robert Underwood who was the verger for 38 years. The inscription reads: 'This garden was made by Robert Underwood, verger 1890–1928. He loved his roses and they loved him.' There are two centenarians recorded on tombstones, one being Elizabeth Young who died in 1919 aged 102 years 2 months. Near the south porch is a tall pillar-like monument to Matthew Greathead who died in 1871 aged 101 years 8 months.

There are also the graves of two Waterloo veterans. Sergeant William Watson died in 1844 aged 57, and on his gravestone is recorded: 'Early in life he entered the Coldstream Guards and fought in the Peninsular War and Waterloo, and subsequently served for some time in the West Indies and retired with a pension. He was a kind, upright and pious man and highly respected.' Augustus Blytheman also fought in the Peninsular War and Waterloo; he served in the 95th Rifle Corps and died in 1847, aged 57.

There is a stone in the churchyard to Robert Willance, erected on the tercentenary of his accident when both horse and rider plunged over Whitcliffe Scar (see Willance's Leap). Another accident brought about the death of Estcourt Sackville Cresswell, who lived with his parents in an apartment over a gunsmith's shop in the Market Place. An explosion occurred in the shop and, although no one was killed at the time, within two weeks two members of the family and a servant had died of shock. Cresswell was a pupil of the grammar school and died on October 30th, 1836, the tomb being erected by his schoolfellows. Behind the church, as you approach from Station Road, is an unmarked gravestone, known as the Plague Stone and probably indicating the communal grave of those who died of the plague between August 1597 and February 1599. The Richmond parish register records 1,072 people dying of the disease within these 19 months, the peak coming in the summer of 1598 with 187 deaths in July and 195 in August.

Church Wynd leads from the churchyard into Frenchgate, a cobbled street of Georgian houses. If you turn right up Frenchgate you arrive at the Green Howards War Memorial at the end of the street, where a series of steps leads up to

*Cornforth Hill, climbing steeply up beside the
castle to the Market Place*

Pottergate. From the top there is a fine view over the town's grey slate roofs to the castle ruins. At the other side of the road, surrounded by trees, is Hill House, home of Frances I'Anson— the *Sweet Lass of Richmond Hill*. The words of the famous song were written by Leonard McNally, an Irish barrister, who married Frances in London in 1787. The poem was set to music by James Hook and performed at Vauxhall Gardens, becoming an immediate success. Frances died in Dublin at the early age of 29. You can return to the Market Place by turning left down Pottergate and then left along Queen's Road and King Street.

NEWBIGGIN, BARGATE AND THE GREEN

FROM the Market Place walk down Finkle Street. This once boasted one of the three bars in the town walls which enclosed an area slightly larger than the Market Place. At the end turn left into Newbiggin, a broad cobbled avenue overlooked by some fine stone houses. The road leads towards Temple Grounds which contain Culloden Tower, built to commemorate the defeat of the 1745 rebellion and standing on the site of Hudswell Peel, a fortified mansion. The grounds are not open to the public. On September 9th, 1558, Richard Snell, a protestant, was burned at the stake in Newbiggen because of his religion. John Wesley preached to a large congregation from the steps of one of the houses. At the Cravengate end is Pear Tree House with a pear tree cut and shaped to its front.

Return back along Newbiggin and turn right down Bargate, a cobbled street descending to the Green. On the right you pass the Board Inn. For many years it had no sign and the entrance was through a shop; it has recently been altered and extended. At the bottom of the road, above the shop on the right, are two sundials dated 1689. Further to the right is the Green shaded by a large and spreading chestnut tree—from the far side there is a pleasant view of the castle keep standing above the roofs of the houses. The road down Bargate continues to Richmond Bridge. There is a fine view downstream of the river Swale tumbling past the ruins of the castle perched on the crag. To return, walk back 50 yards up the hill and turn right up the cobbled lane with a flagged path. Cornforth Hill climbs steeply up beside the castle and passes through an old archway. Bear right at the top into the Market Place.

RIVERSIDE WALK

FROM the bottom end of the Market Place turn right along Millgate. The road descends to the river—don't bear right on to the Castle Walk. As you go down the hill a fine view unfolds of the Swale dropping over a 12 foot rock step. In summer it makes a fine playground for the children; there are toilets and a car park. You can turn right along the riverside to Richmond Bridge or turn left across the grass covered Batts to Station Road.

The waterfall, Riverside Walk

RICHMOND BEACON

TWO miles from the town, just off the road to Marske, is Richmond Beacon. It stands about 50 yards from the road straddling a wall, with five tiers of stone carrying the metal, drum-like, beacon in a cradle. It is situated 1,025 feet above sea level with a fine panoramic view eastwards — on a clear day it is possible to see York Minster to the south-east, and the Cleveland hills and Teesside. The beacon has been a signalling station from early times, fires being lit here to warn the people of danger. During the Spanish Armada it received the warning signal from Roseberry Topping, above Guisborough, and passed it on to the north-western part of Richmondshire and the Bishopric of Durham. It was manned again in the 19th century when the Napoleonic invasion threatened. The last occasion the beacon was used was during the Queen's Silver Jubilee celebrations in 1977.

WILLANCE'S LEAP

ABOUT half a mile further along the Marske road is a squeeze stile on the left after passing the plantation on the right and before the radio masts. Bear slightly to the right through it and across the field to a gateway, just beyond which are two monuments commemorating Willance's Leap. They are set on top of Whitcliffe Scar. Robert Willance, the son of a Richmond grocer, was a successful lead miner who loved to explore the Swaledale hills. In 1606 he was out hunting with a party when they were caught in fog. As they approached the top of the scar his horse leapt forward and careered over the 200 foot high cliff. The horse was killed outright but Robert Willance escaped with a broken leg, which unfortunately had to be amputated. Tradition says that the leg was buried in the churchyard at Richmond, and that Willance was reunited with it when he died on February 12th, 1615. There is a fine view of the Swale flowing between steep wooded hillsides. The monument can also be reached on Walk 3.

EASBY

DOWNSTREAM from Richmond are Easby Abbey and St. Agatha's church. The ruins of the abbey stand beside the Swale in a peaceful wooded valley. They can be reached by a pleasant walk beside the river (see Walk 2) or by road after turning right off the B6271. The road passes a row of old stone almshouses with a plaque on the wall: 'This Hospitall was Founded and Endowed by WILLIAM SMITH RECTOR of MEISONBY in the 83rd year of his age, Anno Domini 1732.' Continue down the hill and the valley opens up disclosing a fine view of the abbey ruins and the parish church.

The abbey was founded for the White Canons by Roald, Constable of Richmond Castle, in 1152 and was later endowed by members of the Scrope family. From the ruins that are left you can visualise the layout. The cloister was not the usual square shape — the southern end is shorter than the northern end and they are not parallel. The building which stands near the road, opposite the church, is the gatehouse.

When the abbey was built the nearby parish church was left untouched. Inside it are several wall paintings — the only finer ones in Yorkshire are at Pickering. On the arches between the aisle and nave are a number of chevrons and there are more wall paintings in the chancel where there is also a replica of the 7th and 8th century Easby Cross. The original stones were found in 1932 and are now in the Victoria and Albert Museum.

THE DRUMMER BOY

THERE is a legend that Easby Abbey and Richmond Castle are connected by an underground passage. When soldiers were stationed in the castle many years ago, it is said they persuaded a young drummer boy to march down a passage they had found in the cellar. He bravely set off down the dark passage, beating his drum. The soldiers above ground could follow the beat, out of the castle and across the streets, until somewhere near the grammar school it suddenly stopped. The drummer boy was never seen again. What happened in that dark passage no one will ever know. But it is said that if you listen on a quiet night you may still hear the young drummer boy beating his drum far underground.

Easby Abbey and St. Agatha's Church

Walks from Richmond

RICHMOND is set amid some fine scenery at the foot of Swaledale. The best way to enjoy this scenery is to walk so that you don't disturb the animals and birds and manage to see many things you would otherwise miss. I have described three walks from Richmond, two beside the river Swale and one to Willance's Leap. For further routes in the area see *Walks in Swaledale* by Geoffrey White (Dalesman Publishing Company).

Walk 1. Billy Bank Woods (2½ miles): From the Market Place walk down New Road into Bridge Street. Turn left, pass the green on your right, cross Richmond Bridge, and turn right along a riverside path. After about 100 yards look back to see the familiar view of the Swale passing under the bridge with the castle perched on the crag—a scene painted by J. M. W. Turner, the famous landscape artist. The path gradually climbs above the river among some fine woodland scenery, and you can soon look down on the Swale as it passes around a long sweeping bend.

The path then descends to a small stream and continues downhill through Billy Bank Woods to a field. This is a delightful woodland walk. Go past the first stile on the right and cross over the next stile so as to continue along the edge of the field and skirt Round Howe on your left. The tree-covered mound is natural; the river may at one time have flowed around the hill making it an island.

The path continues to a footbridge across the river where there is a picnic site. Cross this bridge and bear left to the main road, then turn right back towards Richmond. You can look across the valley to Billy Bank Woods through which you have just passed. As you enter Richmond keep an eye open for the sign on your left which reads: 'Solar Eclipse, June 1927—centre line for totality.' Bear right down Cravengate, then turn left along Newbiggen and return to the Market Place along Finkle Street.

Walk 2.   Easby (2¼ miles): From the Market Place walk down Station Road past the parish church. Turn left along the first lane beyond the church and then right at the junction. The track climbs gradually into the wood. There is a fine view of the river Swale at the top and upstream you can look over Mercury Bridge to the castle ruins. Continue along the track until it splits near a white gate; turn right along the riverside path — you can return along the path in front of you.

When the track turns left to a house, continue straight on beside the river and cross the stile into a pleasant wood. The path continues through the wood to another stile and a series of steps; turn right at the top and you can see the ruins of Easby Abbey. Cross another stile and continue along the edge of the field, above the river. Cross the stile beside the gate and bear right around the Abbey Mill buildings. On your right, after passing the stile, you can see the sluice gate which allowed water to reach the mill.

The entrance to Easby Abbey and the parish church are both on the left of the path. To return to Richmond go back along the track as far as the concrete steps, but instead of descending the steps keep straight ahead beside the wall. The path carries straight on, passing a sports field on the right, to the junction near the white gate which you passed earlier. Continue along the track, and then turn back left into Station Road and right to the Market Place.

Walk 3.   Willance's Leap (6½ miles from Richmond, 4 miles from Whitcliffe Farm): This walk can be started from Richmond, but you can save 2½ miles of road walking by driving along Westfields. From the Market Place go down Finkle Street and turn left along Newbiggen. Turn right up Cravengate and bear right at the sub post office up Westfields. Continue along the road for a mile, with some pleasant views on the left. If you are driving along the road park near Whitcliffe Farm.

Carry on along the road, passing above High Leases Farm. After 200 yards the path goes through a gate into the wood, giving occasional pleasant views of the river Swale through the trees on the left. Depending on the season you may see primroses, forget-me-nots or wild roses. At the end of the wood cross a stile into a field. On the crag top on your right you can see the monuments at Willance's Leap which you will pass later on the walk.

Continue on the track across the field and fork right along a grass track, indicated by a yellow arrow, just before reaching a farm. Pass over a stile. Keep the next farm buildings on your left and continue to a gate at the end of the field which leads to a tarmac road. Cross the road, and keeping the stone wall on your left, head for a stile in a stone wall. Cross the stile and continue over the field to a stile near a gate which leads to a tarmac road. Turn right up the tarmac road, turn left at the junction and cross over a cattle grid; the tarmac road then swings right into Deepdale.

Monument at Willance's Leap

Continue up the valley and twenty yards before the cattle grid at the head of the dale turn back sharp right along the top of the valley and follow the wall along the cliff top. There are some fine views, firstly into Deepdale and then across Swaledale. The path swings left and heads for Willance's Leap, where you pass the two monuments which you earlier saw from the wood. Continue over two stiles and then straight on along the edge of a field to pass some gorse bushes and reach a gate. At this point there is a fine view over the Vale of Mowbray to the Cleveland hills. On the right, across the valley, is the village of Hudswell; on the left is Richmond Beacon. Pass through the gate and follow the track which curves right to High Leases Farm. Turn left back to your car or continue down the road back to Richmond.

RICHMOND is a fine touring centre situated on the edge of the Yorkshire Dales National Park, with Swaledale, Wensleydale and Teesdale being easily accessible from the town. There are also a number of interesting villages around Richmond.

Reeth, Swaledale: The stone houses are gathered around a spacious green which is crossed by the main road. The village can be approached from Richmond by either the B6270, which goes through the fine wooded valley, or the hill road which passes Richmond Beacon and Willance's Leap. There is an interesting museum, just off the green, with exhibits showing the vanishing way of life of the Dales people and many relics of the lead mining which used to be undertaken in the area.

Keld, Swaledale: This hamlet, at the head of Swaledale, is a paradise for anyone who is prepared to walk a couple of miles. Close to it are a number of waterfalls—Catrake and Wainwath Forces on the river Swale and Kisdon Force on East Gill. From the track near Kisdon Force there is a fine view of the gorge carved out by the Swale as it flows between Rogan Seat, 2,204 feet, and Kisdon, 1,636 feet. The Pennine Way passes close to the hamlet.

Tan Hill Inn and Arkengarthdale: Just beyond Keld the road climbs steeply up through West Stonesdale and on to Stonesdale Moor. Near the road junction, on the moor top, is Tan Hill Inn—the highest in Britain. It is 1,732 feet above sea level and originally served miners at the nearby coal mines. The coal was transported by pack horse and wagons to Swaledale, Arkengarthdale and Kirkby Stephen. The road continues down Arkengarthdale to Reeth where you can return to Richmond. The hillsides around the valley have been scarred by mining, but nature has overtaken the disused mines and today it is a pleasant drive over the moors past the strange-sounding hamlets of Whaw and Booze. The C. B. Hotel takes its name from Charles Bathurst who owned the local lead mines—every pig of lead bore his initials.

Wensleydale: The dale is easily accessible from Richmond. The A6108 passes down the wooded banks of the river Swale and then climbs over Barden Moor to Leyburn, set at the foot of Wensleydale.

Aysgarth, Wensleydale: The village is noted for its three fine waterfalls on the river Ure. The road passes over a bridge giving fine views of Upper Force, and from the car park you can walk downstream to Middle Force and Lower Force. The falls are spectacular after heavy rain. There is a carriage museum in the mill, near the bridge, and an information centre in the car park.

Hardraw, Wensleydale: The village is about a mile from Hawes. Behind the Green Dragon Inn is Hardraw Force, a waterfall which makes a 100 foot dive from the rim of a ravine into a rock pool. A path passes along one side of the ravine, round the back of the waterfall, and returns along the other side. It is the highest unbroken fall of water, above ground, in England.

Buttertubs Pass: Close to Hardraw is the Buttertubs Pass which crosses the ridge between Swaledale and Wensleydale at a height of 1,726 feet. At the top of this wild, unfenced moorland road are a number of deep chasms—these are the Buttertubs from which the pass takes its name. The pass can be used to combine a fine circular tour of Wensleydale and Swaledale.

Bolton on Swale: Situated in the Vale of Mowbray only six miles from Richmond is this pleasant village. Close to the main road is the village pump but the most interesting feature is the grave of Henry Jenkins. The 10 foot high monument commemorates his death in 1670 aged 169 years.

There is also an inscribed plaque inside the church to this super centenarian, who, when he was 100, used to swim across the nearby river Swale.

Scorton: An attractive village of stone-built houses in the Vale of Mowbray. The road skirts the large green which contains a cricket pitch.

Ravensworth: Five miles north of Richmond is this interesting village. The houses stand around a green, on which is the base of a stone cross. On the outskirts is a ruined castle, once the home of the Fitzhughs.

Kirby Hill: Stands on a ridge overlooking Ravensworth. There are a number of old stone houses gathered around a green, one bearing the date 1678 above the doorway. There are some good views from the edge of the village across the river Tees into Durham.

Barnard Castle and Teesdale: A fine excursion can be made from Richmond to Teesdale. Barnard Castle has the magnificent Bowes Museum on the outskirts and the ruins of the 11th century castle overlooking the river Tees. About two miles downstream are the ruins of Egglestone Abbey which were immortalised by Sir Walter Scott. The road into Teesdale passes through the picturesque villages of Lartington, Cotherstone and Romaldkirk. Further up the dale is the spectacular High Force, set in a wooded ravine. Two miles downstream is the less well-known Low Force, where picturesque Winch Bridge crosses the river Tees.